Structured Analysis Of Competing Hypotheses

Theory And Application

Analytic Methodologies Project

Diane E. Chido – Editor-in-Chief
Richard M. Seward, Jr. – Assistant Editor
Katrina M. Altman – Technical Writer
James J. Kelly – Technical Writer

Kristan J. Wheaton – Project Supervisor

Inspired by the ideas of Jim Breckenridge, Chairman, Department of Intelligence Studies, Mercyhurst College.

© 2006
Mercyhurst College Institute of Intelligence Studies Press

Table Of Contents

Introduction

"What people perceive, how readily they perceive it, and how they process this information after receiving it are all strongly influenced by past experience, education, cultural values, role requirements, and organizational norms, as well as by the specifics of the information received. This process may be visualized as perceiving the world through a lens or screen that channels and focuses and thereby may distort the images that are seen."
– Richards J. Heuer, Jr., Psychology of Intelligence Analysis [1]

Intelligence analysis is both a science and an art. Analysts are engaged in estimating the likelihood of future events that may save or imperil thousands. Those of us dependent on such estimates sleep better imagining that the analytic process is as exacting and methodical as science. However, the future is ever evolving and the degree of certainty with which we can "know" it is in constant flux.

Mindsets and mental models help us in breaking down the world into smaller pieces that we can accept or reject and allow us to quickly understand these pieces as they relate to the whole. This enables us to deal with the vast information flow that constantly bombards us, using an almost involuntary shorthand. However, this process, once intended to let us know if we should run from a saber-toothed tiger or scratch him behind the ears, can lead to severe lapses in judgment when creating an intelligence product in the Internet age.

As Malcolm Gladwell explains in his bestselling book, *Blink: The Power of Thinking Without Thinking*,[2] our first impressions and intuitive judgments are appropriate when choosing among seven different varieties of jam in the supermarket. However, in assessing Saddam Hussein's intentions over the next three years, we need to rely on more scientific methods. We can train our "adaptive unconscious," or the part of our minds that allows us to make such quick decisions, to work more effectively, especially in terms of our particular field of expertise. An intelligence analyst on the Iraq desk can much better assess the meaning of Saddam suddenly departing Baghdad for Tikrit at 4 a.m., than the jam salesman, but even as the desk officer considers the possibilities, he would benefit greatly from a tested methodology to organize his thoughts.

Richards Heuer is more direct. As he points out in *Psychology of Intelligence Analysis*,[3] "...simple rules of thumb are often useful in helping us deal with complexity and ambiguity. Under many circumstances, however, they lead to predictably faulty judgments known as cognitive biases."[4]

Analysis of Competing Hypotheses (ACH) is an analytic methodology based on the principles of the scientific method. Using it forces the analyst to set aside his mental model and look for inconsistencies in the data that may indicate a flaw in the model or deception on the part of the target. This method enables the analyst to shatter the lens of perception by attempting to disprove a number of hypotheses, rather than let his mind jump to conclusions and permit biases and mindsets to determine that "I've seen this before" or "This is a clear case of..."

Structured Analysis of Competing Hypotheses (SACH) takes ACH further and deeper, adding structure and automation that permit the analyst to go beyond his first estimate and discover not only what he does not know, but also what he *can* know with a reasonable degree of certainty. SACH is a scientific base for creating the art form that is an intelligence product. SACH enables the analyst to keep track of a large amount of data; it saves the time that made manual ACH unworkable in many instances. SACH permits managers to follow analyst's progress quickly and clearly. It enables decisionmakers to view options that the analyst considered and rejected and to follow the analyst's logic used to arrive at one estimate over another. SACH also improves oversight, providing an audit trail that evaluators can quickly trace to understand how the analyst reached the estimate.

Not only must the analysis be sound to provide an effective intelligence product, but the analyst must also present it in a manner that the decisionmaker will act upon it. SACH ensures that the analyst knows which pieces of evidence are the keys to the estimate, and the structure helps the analyst place these bottom line items right up front so the decisionmaker cannot miss them. SACH provides the improvements to the intelligence process decisionmakers want and need to prepare effectively for future threats or to take advantage of future opportunities.

Chapter 1: What *Is* Intelligence?

*"...all attempts to develop ambitious theories of
intelligence have failed."*
– *Walter Laquer, A World of Secrets: The Uses and Limits
of Intelligence*[5]

There is no consistent, universal definition of
intelligence. Despite the fact that the field of intelligence
in various forms has existed since there have been modern
states, the Intelligence Community (IC) has yet to accept a
standard term.

This is particularly important as intelligence
professionals enter the 21st Century. In previous times,
intelligence could reasonably be defined by "secrets" –
something kings and princes had and something that could
be stolen by clever spies and agents. Information of use to
these leaders was generally located in the minds and courts
of other leaders.

This is no longer true. It is no longer enough to
steal secrets. Collection of information has become an
almost trivial exercise and most people complain of
information overload rather than a lack of information. The
location of useful information has also changed. It has

become more dispersed geographically and generally reliable open sources often contain as much valuable information to a specific decisionmaker as secret ones.

The explosion of data as a result of the growth of the Internet in the 1990s and the convergence of wireless voice and data communication in this decade are also dramatically changing the way information is received and used. It is no longer good enough to define intelligence as "secret stealing." There are still important secrets to steal but this is only one part of a much-enlarged mission.

Exacerbating this problem is the advent of Business and Law Enforcement Intelligence functions. These relatively recent additions make it imperative that the concept of intelligence has a general definition – one that can apply in all three circumstances: business, law enforcement, and national security. Failure to establish such a definition, or using three different definitions, calls into question the validity of the very concept of "intelligence." Without such a broad-based definition, intelligence, literally, does not exist.

This has not been the approach of either the intelligence community itself or those charged with oversight. In fact, the acts that have established the modern intelligence community contain little of real use in defining the essence of intelligence.

The Intelligence Reform and Terrorism Prevention Act of 2004 is the most comprehensive overhaul of the IC since its creation by the National Security Act of 1947.

Despite altering the structure of the IC, the 2004 Act fails to completely define intelligence:

> "The terms 'national intelligence' and 'intelligence related to national security' refer to all intelligence, regardless of the source from which derived and including information gathered within or outside the United States, that (A) pertains, as determined consistent with any guidance issued by the President, to more than one United States Government agency; and (B) that involves (i) threats to the United States, its people, property, or interests (ii) the development, proliferation, or use of weapons of mass destruction (iii) or any other matter bearing on United States national or homeland security."[6]

Abstracted to its simplest form, the law states that "intelligence refers to intelligence that pertains to more than one US agency and involves threats, the use of weapons of mass destruction or any other matter bearing on security." The idea that "intelligence refers to intelligence" is not terribly useful. The clause regarding "more than one agency" is confusing and seems to allow bureaucrats a loophole that will inhibit the sharing of information. Finally, the focus on threats and security seems misplaced as well. Surely the US intelligence community is also responsible for identifying opportunities as well?

In contrast, the 1947 Act split intelligence into two components, "foreign intelligence" and "counterintelligence"[7]:

"Foreign intelligence" was defined as information relating to the capabilities, intentions, or activities of foreign governments or elements thereof; foreign organizations, or foreign activities, or international terrorist activities.

"Counterintelligence" referred to information gathered, and activities conducted to protect against espionage, other intelligence activities, sabotage, or assassinations conducted by or on behalf of foreign governments or elements thereof, foreign organizations, or foreign persons, or international terrorist activities."

This definition, in contrast, reflects the historic, secrets-based notion of intelligence with its focus on "information." As stated previously, most decisionmakers believe they have too much information. The current problem is not collection of additional information; rather, it is to make sense of the information already available. This requires analysis, a critical function of all modern intelligence units, but a function that goes unmentioned in either the 2004 or 1947 definition.

More importantly, these definitions give no indication of what intelligence is designed to do. What exactly is the purpose of intelligence? Perhaps sensing this lack of purpose, other writers have broadened the definition over the years.

Following the National Security Act of 1947, Sherman Kent, a groundbreaking contributor to intelligence analysis, constructed his own definitions of intelligence which appear in his influential book, *Strategic Intelligence for American World Policy:*

"Intelligence is knowledge." [8]

"Intelligence is an institution; it is a physical organization of living people which pursues the special kind of knowledge at issue." [9]

"In the language of the trade, the word intelligence is used not merely to designate the types of knowledge [discussed] and the organization to produce this knowledge, it is used as a synonym for the *activity* which the organization performs." [10]

Kent spearheaded the effort to define intelligence, but his definitions remain too vague for practical use. He noted that intelligence is more than just information pertinent to national security; either foreign or domestic, adding that it is both an organization and a process.

However, these descriptions remain incomplete. Even as Kent states that "intelligence is knowledge," not all knowledge is intelligence. Not all knowledge helps a decisionmaker make decisions. In the current lingo, not all knowledge is "actionable". In addition to relevance, intelligence must also be estimative. It must address the decisionmaker's need to know not what has happened, but what is likely to happen.

The process component of intelligence that Kent first introduced is the basis for the definitions of experienced intelligence analysts, Mark Lowenthal and

Robert Clark. Lowenthal, a twenty-seven year intelligence veteran with both the government and the private sector, and serving as vice chairman of the National Intelligence Council for Evaluation, and performing the duties of the Assistant Director of Central Intelligence for Analysis and Production in 2002[11], constructed a definition of intelligence that focuses on the process function of intelligence:

> "Intelligence is the process by which specific types of information important to national security are requested, collected, analyzed, and provided to policymakers; the products of that process; the safeguarding of these processes and this information by counterintelligence activities; and the carrying out of operations as requested by lawful authorities."[12]

Moreover, Lowenthal argues that information, which decisionmakers request, provides a foundation upon which the intelligence process can be based:

> "Intelligence refers to information that meets the stated or understood needs of policymakers and has been collected, refined, and narrowed to meet those needs. Intelligence is a subset of the broader category of information; intelligence and the entire process by which it is identified, obtained, and analyzed, respond to the needs of policymakers. All intelligence is information; not all information is intelligence."[13]

Unlike Lowenthal, Robert Clark, a retired electronics and intelligence officer with the US Air Force, and a CIA analyst and executive in the intelligence directorate, claims that intelligence "is about reducing uncertainty in conflict."[14] Clark also suggests that the definition of intelligence include actionable information:

> "…The primary customer of intelligence is the person who will act on the information – the executive, the decisionmaker, the combat commander, or the law enforcement officer. Writers therefore describe intelligence as being *actionable* information." Not all actionable information is intelligence, however."[15]

Adding to Kent's definition of intelligence as knowledge, Clark states that intelligence must be information upon which consumers can act. Clark also emphasizes that open source information should not be excluded from intelligence activities. Many types of unclassified sources provide excellent intelligence including United Nations and other non-governmental organization reports, press releases, news articles, and academic journals.

Finally, Clark's definition includes one vital component that had been left out of other definitions. He states that consumers of intelligence include not only those in national security, but decisionmakers from the law enforcement field: Federal Bureau of Investigation, Drug Enforcement Agency, Alcohol Tobacco and Firearms, state and local police, and other agencies, both federal and state, all conduct their own types of intelligence analysis and products. Federal, state, and local police compile information into databases detailing criminal patterns and violence.

In today's market-oriented world, competitive, or business intelligence must also be considered when defining intelligence. Competitive intelligence is defined as:

> "... a systematic program for gathering and analyzing information about your competitors' activities and general business trends to further your own company's goals."[16]

In the corporate world, competitive intelligence is an extremely important component of a company's survival. It allows managers to reduce uncertainty by identifying surprises, threats, and opportunities, to improve long- and short-term planning, and to gain a competitive advantage. Using the intelligence gathered, firms can anticipate changes in both their competitors and the marketplace, discover and develop new technologies, and finally, identify new challenges.[17]

Toward A New Definition Of Intelligence

In December 2004, Congress established the Directorate of National Intelligence (DNI), restructuring the IC and placing its once disparate organizations and activities under a central leadership. Upon signing the new law, President Bush stated,

> "The DNI will have the authority to order the collection of new intelligence, to ensure the sharing of information among agencies and to establish common standards for the intelligence community's personnel."[18]

In order to create common standards for the intelligence community, an obvious first step is to adopt a common definition of "intelligence." Analysts, collectors, and policymakers, at all levels, must realize that the term "intelligence" is a very general term which includes all different types of information, organizations, processes, and sources.

Mercyhurst College Institute of Intelligence Studies (MCIIS) advocates the following working definition. The Institute does not claim that this is the best possible definition of modern intelligence but only that it is a step forward on the road to such a definition and, for the purpose of studying Structured Analysis of Competing Hypotheses, it is sufficient.

Thus, intelligence is:

- A process
- Focused externally
- Designed to reduce the level of uncertainty
- For a decisionmaker
- Using information derived from all sources.

These five components are applicable to intelligence analysts in national security, law enforcement, or competitive business intelligence.

The first element: "process," is almost as vague as "intelligence" itself. However, it is clear that intelligence is some sort of process. But what kind?

Lowenthal and Clark have each provided conceptual models of the intelligence process. The Intelligence Cycle described by Lowenthal consists of six continuous steps, starting with the planning and direction stage, followed by collection, then processing and exploitation, analysis, production, and dissemination. This cyclical model (see Figure 1.1) has been widely accepted in the intelligence community as an original attempt to illustrate the process as it actually functions.[19] However, Clark argues that "the traditional cycle may adequately describe the structure and function of an intelligence community, but it does not describe the intelligence process."[20] This is primarily because the traditional intelligence cycle does not allow for new inputs, it is vulnerable to adversarial countermeasures, and because decisionmakers rarely offer feedback.[21]

Figure 1.1
The Traditional Intelligence Cycle[22]

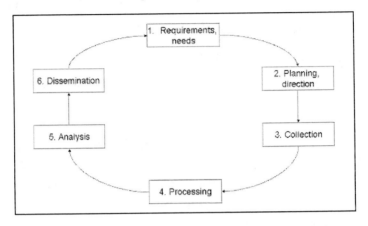

Clark's proposed model, the Target-Centric Approach (see Figure 1.2), focuses all of the inputs on a specified, common target. The target is the subject on which a decisionmaker requests an estimate, and all of the participants – collectors, analysts, and producers – coordinate their efforts to provide the estimate. Without decisionmaker feedback and a real effort to break down barriers among agencies and change information-sharing guidelines, this approach will also remain a hypothetical model.

After looking at these two processes, which is the one that correctly supports the definition? The answer is neither and both. Each model has its supporters, but shortcomings prevent either approach from becoming universally accepted. It remains clear that intelligence is a process, but researchers have yet to discover a coherent way to illustrate it.

Figure 1.2
Clark's Target-Centric Model Of Intelligence Cycle[23]

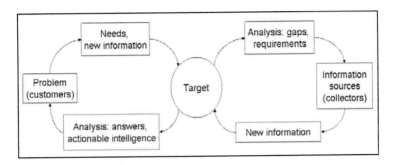

The second element of the MCIIS definition is that intelligence is "focused externally." All consumers of intelligence: governments, agencies, companies, etc., rely on information that concerns issues beyond their own organizations. The point here is that the function of running the organization and the function of scanning the horizon for threats and opportunities are fundamentally different concerns.

One of the earliest intelligence functions was to scout terrain for military movements. The scout's purpose was to draw a map for the commander that indicated not only where the enemy was located (threats) but also where the way was clear (opportunities). These scouts did not get to interfere with the commander's organization or the running of his command, nor did they get to pick the route over the map that the scout had drawn. The scout evaluated the environment and the commander ran his unit and made decisions about where it was to go.

Furthermore, intelligence professionals need to be careful about crossing the policymaking line. It is hard enough to be cognizant of all of the threats and opportunities in the environment surrounding an organization. Trying to also come to a conclusion about the best course of action for a particular organization (and the degree of knowledge about the organization itself that this implies) is probably ill-advised. Perhaps the most embarrassing recent incident of crossing the line between policy and intelligence was George Tenet's blatant selling of the intelligence regarding Weapons of Mass Destruction (WMD) in Iraq ("It's a slam dunk!"[24]) combined with the WMD Commission's finding that this conclusion was "...dead wrong."[25] If intelligence is not focused externally, then one is not doing intelligence.

All intelligence is designed to reduce uncertainty about a certain subject; otherwise, it would just be information. It is the analytic process that creates intelligence from information.[26] Analysts are not fortune-tellers, however. There is always some uncertainty in any estimate that intelligence professionals develop. The best that the decisionmaker can reasonably ask for is that intelligence reduces his or her level of uncertainty.

Likewise, intelligence is produced for a decisionmaker. It is this focus on the decisionmaker that distinguishes intelligence from other types of reporting. This focus on the decisionmaker means that the intelligence professional must consider the decisionmaker's needs – a deputy secretary in charge of nuclear nonproliferation might have little use for a report on crop yields in Burkina

Faso, for example. This does not mean that the intelligence professional says what the decisionmaker wants to hear. No one likes to hear bad news but, if an analyst is to maintain his or her credibility over the long haul, the analyst must sometimes provide unpopular estimates.

In addition, the intelligence professional has an obligation to not only answer questions the decisionmaker asks but also to answer questions the decisionmaker *should have* asked. The intelligence professional's job is to know the environment outside the organization better than anyone else. Imagine if our commander asks his scout to discover the easiest road for his horses to travel. The scout comes back, reports and the troop sets off down the recommended road only to find that there is a raging river and the bridge is out. It will do the scout little good to complain, "You only asked me about the road!"

This focus on the decisionmaker is also where the justification for secrecy, or at least confidentiality, becomes an implied part of the definition. Many people think of intelligence as a secret activity. This is not necessarily so and, even if it was, it would not be secrecy for secrecy's sake. No, the secrecy implied in this definition is for the benefit of the decisionmaker, to give him or her time to think, plan, and act, or to preserve those sources and methods that will give him or her good intelligence in the future.

The last important element of intelligence is that "information is derived from all sources." Information used in reports aimed at reducing uncertainty does not necessarily need to come from intercepted secret communications or covert actions. Rather, information from all sources including imagery intelligence, measurement and signatures intelligence, signals intelligence, human intelligence, and open source intelligence all contribute to intelligence. Open source information including newspapers, journals, press releases, Internet sources, academia, and other reports are indispensable sources of information once they have been fully validated and tested for reliability.

Chapter 2: Words Of Estimative Probability

"In addition to conveying disagreements, analysts must also find ways to explain to policymakers degrees of certainty in their work. Some publications we have reviewed use numerical estimates of certainty, while others rely on phrases such as "probably" or "almost certainly." We strongly urge that such assessments of certainty be used routinely and consistently throughout the Community. Whatever device is used to signal the degree of certainty – mathematical percentages, graphic representations, or key phrases – all analysts in the Community should have a common understanding of what the indicators mean and how to use them."
– Commission On The Intelligence Capabilities Of The United States Regarding Weapons Of Mass Destruction[27]

Current debates in Washington seek to assign blame for the "intelligence failure" preceding the 9/11 terrorist attacks. This stems from the declassification of information that was available prior to the terrorist attack, which might have prevented al Qaeda from implementing its plans. At the forefront is a partially declassified Presidential Daily Brief (PDB) from 6 August 2001, titled, "Bin Ladin Determined to Strike in US."

In the memo (Annex 1), intelligence analysts at the CIA attempted to provide estimative judgments on the probability of bin Ladin attacking United States territory. However, the language used in the memo lacks words of estimative probability (WEP) that reduce uncertainty, thus preventing the President and his decisionmakers from implementing measures directed at stopping al Qaeda's actions. A White House press release on 10 April 2004 claimed that there was no information that offered a clear warning of the 9/11 attack: "The only recent information concerning possible current activities in the PDB related to two incidents. There is no information that either incident was related to the 9-11 [sic] attacks."[28] In addition, President Bush explained to the 9/11 Commission that, "the intelligence did not specify a time or a place for an attack, but if his administration had known more, it would have taken every action to thwart the al Qaeda terrorists."[29]

So how could an intelligence report prepared by the CIA for the President of the United States not contain an estimate of what is likely to happen in the near future, especially on such a critical issue? Why did this memo, which seems to serve as a warning in hindsight, not move anyone in the government to prepare for the events on 9/11? A simple answer to this question is that the lack of words of estimative probability failed to cause decisionmakers to perceive a direct threat that required action. Instead, the memo contains less expressive words that convey no valuable estimative judgments:

"Al Qaeda members -- including some who are U.S. citizens -- have resided in or traveled to the U.S. for years, and the group apparently maintains a support structure that could aid attacks.[30]

And,

"The millennium plotting in Canada in 1999 *may have been* part of bin Ladin's first serious attempt to implement a terrorist strike in the US."

What exactly do "apparently" and "may have been" mean in terms of probability? Do they reduce any uncertainty as to whether al Qaeda is planning an imminent attack? Claiming that bin Ladin "apparently" maintains a support structure that *could* aid attacks does nothing to reduce uncertainty about whether or not he actually will launch an attack in the near future. "Apparently" only tells the reader that there is a possibility that al Qaeda has some means at its disposal, but nothing about capability or tactical plans. In addition, "may have been" is vague enough to give every reader a unique interpretation as to the alleged connection between the millennium plot and bin Ladin.

As professionals trained to make estimative judgments, analysts must be able to convey, with confidence, the probability of an event occurring when preparing an intelligence product. One long-established method was conceived by Sherman Kent, one of the greatest contributors to the intelligence analysis field. In 1964, Kent published a classified CIA report attempting to quantify the qualitative judgments made by intelligence analysts. Kent attempted to "set forth the community's findings in such a way as to make clear to the reader what is certain knowledge and what is reasoned judgment, and within this large realm of judgment what varying degrees of certitude lie behind each key statement."[31]

Kent argued that although "practically all substantive intelligence people constantly make estimates,"[32] analysts do not convey a level of confidence or probability in their estimates that allows decisionmakers the ability to come to a definite or actionable conclusion. For example, in March 1951, National Intelligence Estimate (NIE) 29-51, pertaining to the probability of an invasion of Yugoslavia by the Soviet Union, concluded that:

> "Although it is impossible to determine which course the Kremlin is likely to adopt, we believe that the extent of Satellite military and propaganda preparations indicates that an attack on Yugoslavia in 1951 should be considered a serious possibility."[33]

Several days after the estimate appeared, the chairman of the State Department Policy Planning Staff asked Kent what kind of odds a "serious possibility" expressed. Stunned by the chairman's question, Kent replied that his personal estimate was that the odds were between 35 and 65 in favor of an attack. Troubled by

> "In between these matters of certainty and impossibility lay the large area of the *possible*." – *Sherman Kent*

the initial question, Kent asked other members on the Board of National Estimates what odds that they had in mind. Each member on the board had somewhat different odds, ranging from 20 percent to 80 percent in favor of an attack. This leads one to wonder what estimative purposes does a word like "possible" serve? This vagueness allows a range of probability such that "it is neither certain to happen nor is its happening an impossibility,"[34] which, in turn, reduces a decisionmaker's ability to determine actions from estimates.

Following Kent's realization that the IC lacked words that would be a verbal equivalent to quantitative Figures, he developed a table in which probabilities expressed as percentages match particular terms. Figure 2.1 illustrates the percentages and their corresponding words or phrases.

Figure 2.1
Kent's Words Of Estimative Probability Expressing Percentages[35]

100% Certainty		
The General Area of Possibility		
93%	Give or take about 6%	Almost Certain
75%	Give or take about 12%	Probable
50%	Give or take about 10%	Chances about even
30%	Give or take about 10%	Probably not
7%	Give or take about 5%	Almost certainly not
0% Impossibility		

After the introduction of this conceptualization of probability to the wider intelligence community, those who opposed it attacked Kent saying, "the most a writer can achieve when working in a speculative area of human affairs is communication in only the broadest general sense."[36] Kent referred to these opponents as "poets" and ultimately appealed to them by introducing a number of synonyms for each of the five orders of probability, expressed in Figure 2.2.

Figure 2.2
Kent's Words Of Estimative Probability[37]

Possible	conceivable could may might perhaps
Almost certain	virtually certain all but certain highly probably highly likely odds (or chances) overwhelming
Probable	likely we believe we estimate
50-50	chances are about even chances a little better (or less) than even improbable unlikely

Probably not	we believe that…not we estimate that…not we doubt, doubtful
Almost certainly not	virtually impossible almost impossible some slight chance highly doubtful

Author Michael Schrage, a senior advisor to Massachusetts Institute of Technology's (MIT) Security Studies Program, criticizes the intelligence community for addressing its shortcomings the wrong way. He advocates that the simplest, most cost-effective innovation for the IC to adopt would be to embrace quantifiable odds, rather than reorganize its structure and appoint an intelligence czar. Attaching numbers to intelligence estimates would force analysts and consumers alike to think carefully about quality, creativity, and accountability of analysis, including a less ambiguous standard of accountability.[38]

Although many of the words in Figure 2.2 clearly express the level of certainty intended, it has become evident over time that some words are less useful than others are. Moreover, according to Schrage, "His [Kent] 'words of estimative probability' proved a rhetorically awkward and ultimately futile exercise in encouraging more disciplined discussions of probability in the analytic community."[39]

However, intelligence analysts and the decisionmakers they support tend to be more comfortable using words rather than numbers to describe how confident they are in their estimates.[40] Through years of experience and practical application, the Mercyhurst College Institute for Intelligence Studies (MCIIS) has narrowed down Kent's original WEP to those that are most "clear in their ambiguity."

Words such as "likely" and "unlikely" are preferred because, although they still convey a sense that the analyst is estimating, they also express a probability that something will have an either greater than 50 percent but less than 100 percent, or a greater than zero but less than fifty percent chance of happening. Other acceptable words include: highly likely, highly unlikely, virtually certain, and virtually uncertain – narrowing down those ranges even further. Figure 2.3 shows the full list of words of estimative probability acceptable from the MCIIS viewpoint.

The words "possible, may, could and might," for instance, are so ambiguous that the probability they express can fall anywhere between the range of one and 99 percent. Other words that MCIIS does not advocate using are "we believe…" "we estimate…" and "we doubt that…" Analysis is created by individuals not organizations. The use of the royal "we" is pretentious at best.

MCIIS particularly rejects the use of the term "50-50." There is no escaping the colloquial meaning of the phrase "50-50." Decisionmakers will equate an estimate of 50-50 with an inept analyst either afraid to make a call or unwilling to request more data to make a useful estimate. Given this perception, it is imperative that analysts not settle on such an ineffective estimate and reevaluate the evidence or the analysis to ensure they can make better judgments with a degree of confidence.

Figure 2.3
MCIIS Words Of Estimative Probability

Italics – Never use
Bold – Use
Normal – Use with caution

Possible	*conceivable* *could* *may* *might* *perhaps*
Almost certain	**virtually certain** **all but certain** *highly probable* **highly likely** **odds [or chances] overwhelming**
Probable	**likely** *we believe* *we estimate*
50-50	*chances about even* chances a little better [or less] than even
Probably not	*we believe that . . . not* *we estimate that . . . not* *we doubt, doubtful* improbable **unlikely**
Almost certainly not	**virtually impossible** **almost impossible** **some slight chance** **highly doubtful**

Using appropriate words of estimative probability is only one step in creating quality intelligence products that reduce uncertainty for decisionmakers. An analyst estimating that "it is likely that China is going to fall into the sea" is making a fairly bold assertion. Is there really a 60 to 80 percent chance that such a catastrophic event will happen? In order to properly evaluate such estimative statements, intelligence professionals and individuals responsible for intelligence oversight must also learn to evaluate intelligence correctly.

Chapter 3: Evaluating Intelligence

"In our post-9/11 hindsight, many factors have been identified that now appear to be indicative of the events that were to come. It appears clear (again in hindsight) that implications of these indicators were missed in some cases because of faulty process..."
– Inderjeet Mani and Gary L. Klein, The MITRE Corporation[41]

Ultimately, intelligence is about reducing the level of uncertainty for a decisionmaker. As discussed, Chapter 2 introduced words of estimative probability (WEP) to show how analysts can use words to produce estimates indicating a degree of certainty. Clearly indicating the likelihood of particular events so that a decisionmaker can determine appropriate action is the analyst's most important role. However, when the analyst conveys a degree of probability, how does a decisionmaker go about evaluating the analyst's work?

Weatherman Analogy

Consider the example of a weatherman who just started a new job at a local news station. He only knows one rule (he is still in weatherman school): if it is sunny today, then it is likely to be sunny tomorrow. Later that day, the boss asks him what the weather will be like tomorrow. The weatherman looks out the window at the sun shining and replies that it is likely to be sunny tomorrow. When the boss wakes up the next day, he sees that it is sunny. Was the weatherman right?

Suppose the boss woke up and it was raining. Was the weatherman's forecast wrong?

When the weatherman walks into the office the next morning (after he predicted sun but woke up to rain), the boss yells at him because the forecast was wrong and now that it is raining, the boss's wife is angry that she has to cancel a family picnic planned for that afternoon. After the boss calms down a bit, the weatherman, humbled, asks the boss how he can improve. The boss instructs him to learn more rules, to which the weatherman agrees, but still does not understand how he could have improved upon his original estimate.

Now consider a bad weatherman who has no idea what he is doing. He also knows only one rule – the same rule that the other weatherman knows. However, this weatherman learned the rule incorrectly – he thinks that if it is sunny today it will likely be raining tomorrow. His boss also wants to know what the forecast is for tomorrow, so the weatherman looks out the window, sees that it is sunny, and predicts that it will rain tomorrow. The next day, the boss gets out of bed and looks out the window to see rain. Was this weatherman right? What if the boss wakes up to a sunny day? Was the weatherman wrong?

After reading both of these examples, one can see there is a problem with using the terms "right" and "wrong" to evaluate an analytic estimate. Analysis is probabilistic; designed to reduce levels of uncertainty, not to eliminate them. "Right" and "wrong" are binary options in what is clearly an analog situation. These words are inadequate when it comes to evaluating intelligence.

Process and Product

Intelligence products are final estimates derived from a process. Analysts create such products in the form of analytic reports and presentations for decisionmakers. Analytic products come in a variety of forms, ranging from Presidential Daily Briefs (PDBs), and National Intelligence Estimates (NIEs), to FBI Intelligence Information Reports (IIRs), financial forecasts, and stock assessments.

Process, on the other hand, is the application of rules. One can draw parallels between processes used in intelligence and the sciences. Mathematicians, for example, frequently associate Bayes's Theorem and Bayesian Inference, developed by Thomas Bayes, an 18th century probability mathematician, with statistical theory and probability determinants. Radford Neal, an expert on Bayesian inference and a statistics professor at the

University of Toronto, describes the process of evaluating situations by expressing uncertainty in terms of probability:[42]

"A Bayesian approach to a problem starts with the formulation of a model that we hope is adequate to describe the situation of interest. We then formulate a *prior* distribution over the unknown parameters of the model, which is meant to capture our beliefs about the situation before seeing the data. After observing some data, we apply Bayes' Rule to obtain a *posterior* distribution for these unknowns, which takes account of both the prior and the data. From this posterior distribution we can compute *predictive* distributions for future observations."

In intelligence analysis, as well as mathematics, the legitimacy of products and processes can be either true or false.

- *True processes* are those that produce generally reliable results and include statistics, tested methodologies, and perhaps even intuition based on experience, similar to the processes often used by Wall Street investment analysts.
- *False processes* are those that produce generally unreliable results and include invalidated methods, such as reading horoscopes, tea leaves, or goat entrails.

Tasseomancy: The Art of Reading Tea Leaves: True or False Process?

Historians can trace the practice of Tasseomancy, the art of reading tea leaves, back thousands of years. This is a form of divination commonly associated with the Gypsies in Eastern Europe and inhabitants of the British Isles. The art of predicating the future underlies the concept of Tasseography by which readers interpret patterns of symbols made by tea leaves. Although there are numerous ways to read tea leaves, a common practice has the client sit at a table with the reader. The client drinks the tea leaving the dregs in the bottom of the cup. Then the reader first turns the cup upside down on a saucer and then back over again. The reader takes the cup and reads the pattern left on the saucer. Various symbols have certain meanings. The reader interprets the shapes and symbols of the tea leaves like the Rorschach Inkblot Test. The proximity of the leaves to the rim of the cup indicates the time frame; leaves closest to the rim represent the immediate future.

Possible Interpretations of Patterns That Resemble:

Aircraft: Journey; if broken means danger of accident; can also mean a rise in status.
Clouds: Trouble; with dots means many problems.
Egg: Good omen
Goat: Be careful of enemies.
Harp: Love or harmony.
Wheel: If complete means good fortune; if broken means disappointments.

Sources:
"The Art Of Reading Tea leaves." Easterntea.com, 2005,
    http://www.easterntea.com/tea/readtea.htm
"Tea Leaf Readings- Tasseography" Crystallinks.com,
2005, http://www.crystallinks.com/tea leaves.html

Napoleon At Waterloo:
True Process, False Product

"This morning we still had ninety chances out of hundred in our favor. Bülow's arrival cost us thirty, but we still have sixty against forty."
    -Napoleon, the Battle of Waterloo 18 June 1815

Before marching into battle the afternoon of 18 June 1815, Napoleon had full confidence in victory over British forces. Napoleon's army at the Battle of Waterloo "was generally considered to be much superior on paper, in terms of quality, experience, homogeneity and even motivation". Napoleon also had nearly one hundred more cannon than the Allied forces. While the Emperor's soldiers might numerically have barely outnumbered Wellington's, the British troops only made up about half of the Allied forces on the rain-soaked field that day, and roughly only half of those troops (one-fourth of the total force) were veterans from previous battles.

Yet even with a superior force, an undoubtedly gifted commander, and a divided and inferior enemy force (Wellington was awaiting reinforcement from the Prussians), the French forces did not carry the day. Historians to this day debate how and why Napoleon did not win, with factors from the rainy weather delaying the French attack, to the size of the field to the superior choice of terrain by Wellington. This list is by no means exhaustive, but drives at the heart of the matter. Napoleon, an experienced, successful general, adopted his tactics at the battle from his distinctive and successful fighting methods, including the use of massed infantry assaults and prolonged artillery bombardments. Napoleon's strategy worked in previous engagements, but for whatever reason, was unsuccessful at Waterloo.

Sources:
Herold, Christopher, J., ed. <u>The Mind Of Napoleon</u>. New York: Colombia University Press, 1955.
Roberts, Andrew. <u>Napoleon & Waterloo</u>. New York: Simon & Schuster, 2001.

- *True products* turn out to be, using 20-20 hindsight, correct in their major conclusions. US intelligence was able to give President Kennedy "true" products regarding assessments of Soviet strategic and conventional force capabilities, which bolstered his ability to make difficult decisions, most notably, the US response to Soviet missiles in Cuba.[43]
- *False products* turn out to be, using 20-20 hindsight, incorrect in their major conclusions. Faulty assessments, such as 2002 and early 2003 reports of large stockpiles of weapons of mass destruction in Iraq, are good examples.

Evaluating intelligence by looking at the product and process individually, rather than collectively, yields four possible results. Figure 3.1 shows the four different combinations of product and processes with T standing for "true" and F for "false":

Figure 3.1

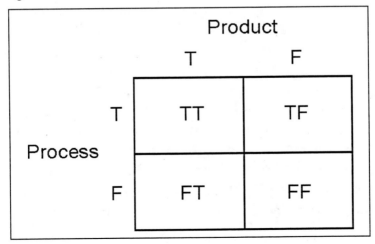

Once an analyst gives an intelligence product to a decisionmaker, it immediately becomes open to evaluation. For obvious reasons, problems rarely arise from cases in which products and process are both true. Typically, false products attract the most attention, even if they arise from true processes.

Which is more important to intelligence: process or product?

Looking back at the two weathermen, the bad weatherman who used the incorrect rule to forecast the weather clearly misapplied the process. Although he might manage to correctly forecast the weather some of the time, the product is less likely to be reliable over time and his estimates will fail more often than not due to this false process.

When the bad weatherman correctly forecasts the weather, the estimate is unlikely to invite evaluation from his boss, who does not have the time to constantly monitor employees who appear to be doing the job "correctly". Eventually, however, the bad weatherman is bound to establish a poor track record and attract negative attention. This situation parallels that of intelligence analysts and decisionmakers, for whom oversight committees review processes and attempt to correct the flaws using recommendations based on postmortem analyses.[44] Much of the public hand wringing at these times revolves around the decisionmaker's concern about the product and, at the other end of the spectrum, the intelligence community's concern about process. As the two polar extremes circle around each other like caged bears, the inextricable link between product and process is lost.

Product and process cannot be separated in intelligence. Because of the probabilistic nature of intelligence, both must be considered in any evaluation of any product – whether true or false. While the focus may shift from one to the other, they are inseparable.

Chapter 4: Analysis Of Competing Hypotheses

*"The DNI should encourage diverse and independent
analysis throughout the Intelligence Community by
encouraging alternative hypothesis generation as part of
the analytic process and by forming offices dedicated to
independent analysis."*
— *Commission On The Intelligence Capabilities Of The
United States Regarding Weapons Of Mass Destruction*[45]

Richards J. Heuer, Jr., a 45-year veteran of the CIA,
claims that "More major intelligence failures have been
caused by failures of analysis than by failures of
intelligence collection."[46] While working at the CIA, for
both the Directorate of Operations and Directorate of
Intelligence, Heuer developed a methodology to improve
the analytic process for generating and evaluating
hypotheses. His method, Analysis of Competing
Hypotheses (ACH), assists analysts in identifying and
questioning basic assumptions and provides a means for
testing hypotheses. ACH consists of an eight-step process
that enables the analyst to formulate multiple hypotheses,
using evidence meant to rule out or *disprove* hypotheses,

while ultimately leaving the single most likely hypothesis. Heuer describes the process as one that is "…grounded in basic insights from cognitive psychology, decision analysis, and the scientific method."[47]

Inherent in all intelligence analyses are cognitive limitations, biases, and mindsets that cause analysts to formulate preconceived assumptions when given incomplete or ambiguous information. These cognitive biases serve as mental short cuts and are subconsciously applied to the evidence through the perceptions, memory, and information processing centers in the mind and occur "prior to and independently of any conscious decision."[48] Recently, the Senate Select Committee on Intelligence's (SSCI) *Report on the U.S. Intelligence Community's Prewar Intelligence Assessments on Iraq* discovered that the use of these assumptions created an unreliable mindset during the intelligence-gathering process, concluding that:

> "The Intelligence Community (IC) suffered from a collective presumption that Iraq had an active and growing weapons of mass destruction (WMD) program. This 'group think' dynamic led Intelligence Community analysts, collectors, and managers to both interpret ambiguous evidence as conclusively indicative of a WMD program as well as ignore or minimize evidence that Iraq did not have active and expanding weapons of mass destruction programs. This presumption was so strong that formalized IC mechanisms established to challenge assumptions and group think were not utilized."[49]

In addition, the SSCI claimed that, "In the case of Iraq's weapons of mass destruction (WMD) capabilities, the Committee found that intelligence analysts, in many cases, based their analysis more on their expectations than on an objective evaluation of the information in the intelligence reporting."[50]

If this is the case, how are analysts to consciously remove biases from their work without impairing their analytic skills? Although developed long before the issue of Iraqi WMD came to the fore, Richards Heuer's eight-step ACH method addresses the concerns of the SSCI by systematically allowing the analyst to develop alternative hypotheses and weigh evidence and explicit assumptions against those hypotheses.

Eight-Step Process Of Analysis Of Competing Hypotheses:[51]

Step 1: Identify the possible hypotheses to be considered. When possible, use a group of analysts with different perspectives to brainstorm the possibilities.

In the first step, it is important to identify all the hypotheses that are relevant to the target. In order to elicit every possibility, a brainstorming session with a group of diverse analysts is recommended to stimulate the imagination and bring out ideas that a lone analyst might not have considered. However, this step can also be performed effectively by an imaginative analyst if there is no time to assemble a team. After identifying all of the potential hypotheses, the analyst then begins narrowing down the choices into the most likely options that can then be examined in greater detail.

When narrowing down possibilities, "it is necessary to distinguish hypotheses that appear to be *disproved* from those that are simply *unproven*."[52] By separating the hypotheses into either category, and using validated evidence, an analyst can eliminate the hypotheses which have been disproved. However, it is imperative that unless evidence clearly disproves a hypothesis, it be kept in play, because, again, the objective is not to accept which hypotheses will be used, but rather, to further investigate only hypotheses that can not be ruled out after all of the information has been evaluated.

There is no correct number of hypotheses that should be suggested and considered[53] after the brainstorming and preliminary evaluation stage. David Osias of the Office of Intelligence, a proponent of ACH, believes that "… discussion of alternative analysis, alternative scenarios, and alternative conclusions is the most powerful way to communicate uncertainty and confidence."[54] Moreover, Heuer suggests that, "As a general rule, the greater your level of uncertainty, or the greater the policy impact of your conclusion, the more alternatives you may wish to consider."[55]
It is important that the hypotheses *compete*; that is, they are largely if not entirely mutually exclusive.

> **Where is the boss going to lunch?**
> **Step 1**
>
> To demonstrate the eight-step process, consider that the local news station's weatherman normally eats lunch at his office every day. Imagine it is nearly noon, and he is hungry, but because he forgot his lunch on the kitchen counter when he left for work, he is forced to eat out at a restaurant. However, he does not want to go to the same place as his boss because he ruined his boss's picnic yesterday when he forecast the weather incorrectly. In addition, he is looking for something inexpensive, but there are only two fast, low-cost restaurants in the area – Burger King and Subway. Unfortunately, he is also aware that the boss only goes to these two restaurants, so he will have to make sure that he chooses the restaurant that his boss does not choose. Thus, the weatherman has determined that there are two possible hypotheses to test in order to avoid his boss:
> - The boss will eat lunch at Subway
> - The boss will eat lunch at Burger King

Step 2: Make a list of significant evidence and arguments for and against each hypothesis.

Evidence used should be interpreted broadly to include all factors *that might have an impact on judgments about the hypotheses*. Analysts should also include assumptions or logical deductions, goals, and standard procedures regarding the target (in this case, the boss's lunchtime location).

In this second step, make a list of all of the general evidence that applies to each hypothesis. Heuer recommends asking these questions for each hypothesis:[56]

- If this hypothesis were true, what should I expect to be seeing or not seeing?
- What are all the things that must have happened, or may still be happening, and of which one should I expect to see evidence?
- If you are not seeing the evidence, why not? Is it because it has not happened, it is not normally observable, it is being concealed from you, or because you or the intelligence collectors have not looked for it?

Where is the boss going to lunch? (Continued...)
Step 2

In the second step, list all the evidence that applies to these competing hypotheses. In order to determine where not to go, consider these five pieces of evidence:
- The boss always buys his lunch.
- There are only two restaurants nearby.
- The boss is thrifty.
- The boss's doctor advised him to avoid fat due to high blood pressure.
- The boss's wife is monitoring his diet.

Step 3: Prepare a matrix with hypotheses across the top row and evidence down the left-hand column. Analyze the "diagnosticity" of the evidence and arguments – that is, identify which items are most helpful in judging the relative likelihood of alternative hypotheses.

The goal of this step is to take the hypotheses from Step 1 and the evidence from Step 2, and put them into a matrix, with the hypotheses listed across the top row and the evidence down the first left-hand column. Then move *across* the table, taking one piece of evidence at a time to determine how consistently it fits with each corresponding hypothesis along the top row. In order to determine evidence fitness, ask yourself whether or not it is consistent with, inconsistent with, or irrelevant to each hypothesis. Then, make the proper notation in the corresponding cell. Notations may consist of pluses, minuses and question marks, or C (consistent), I (inconsistent), and N/A (not applicable), or any other logical coding. Repeat this process for each cell in the matrix until all of the cells are marked.

Constructing a matrix allows the analyst to individually weigh the diagnosticity of each piece of evidence, which, according to Heuer, "is a key difference between analysis of competing hypotheses and traditional analysis."[57] By examining the diagnosticity, analysts can eliminate evidence shared by more than one hypothesis, which is not useful in proving or disproving any hypotheses and therefore, has no diagnostic value. Additional notations in each cell can also be made if the analyst wants to show the intrinsic importance of each piece of evidence, or the ease with which items of evidence might be concealed or manipulated when the probability of deception or denial is a serious concern.[58] For example, an analyst can weigh the evidence depending upon the level of confidence the analyst has in the reliability and validity of the source. Notations for weight are most easily assigned H (high), M (medium), and L (low).

Step 3 is the most critical in the eight-step process and it is essential that the analyst pay careful attention to this step because it differs most from the natural, intuitive style of traditional analysis.

Where is the boss going to lunch? (Continued...)
Step 3

After gathering the evidence, construct a matrix which displays the hypothetical options as to where the boss will go to lunch across the top row. Then place each piece of evidence in its own cell down the first left-hand column. Next, evaluate each piece of evidence while moving *across* the rows as it corresponds with the hypothesis at the top of the column (*see Figure 4.1*). For the first piece of evidence, "boss always buys his lunch," both Burger King and Subway are marked with "+" because it does not exclude either option. In addition, that evidence is weighted "low" because the "boss always buys his lunch" is unimportant and holds little value for determining whether he will go to either Burger King or Subway. However, for the second piece of evidence, "boss's wife monitors his diet", Burger King is marked with "-" and Subway with "+", as Subway offers more low-fat menu items. Also, the weight of the "boss's wife monitoring his diet" is marked "high" because it is an important piece of evidence in determining where the boss will go to lunch. Continue this process for each of the remaining pieces of evidence.

Note that "boss always buys his lunch" and "only two restaurants nearby" are both marked with plus signs because this evidence fits with either hypothesis.

Figure 4.1

Where is the boss going to lunch?			
	Weight	Burger King	Subway
Boss always buys his lunch	L	+	+
Wife is monitoring his diet	H	-	+
Boss is thrifty	M	-	+
Dr. advises boss to eat right	H	-	+
Only two restaurants nearby	L	+	+

Step 4: Refine the matrix. Reconsider the hypotheses and delete evidence and arguments that have no diagnostic value.

In this stage, reconsider or reword hypotheses in order to reflect all significant alternatives. Some hypotheses may need to be combined into one, or one hypothesis may need to be separated into two. Also, the analyst should cross out or otherwise remove from view evidence from the matrix that is unimportant or has no diagnostic value, as discussed in the previous step. The analyst should never delete evidence since, while it may not serve a purpose in simple ACH, this evidence might be critical in structured ACH.

Following the construction of the matrix in step 3, it is now time to refine and modify the hypotheses and evidence that can be either (a) ruled out or (b) combined or separated. In Figure 4.2, three instances are highlighted in which the evidence provides no diagnostic value to either hypothesis.

After identifying the evidence that is no longer needed, indicate that it is no longer relevant for the current analysis. Figure 4.2 notes that "boss always buys his lunch" and "only two restaurants nearby" were given pluses for each hypothesis. They do not support or refute either hypothesis, and are no longer relevant for a

Figure 4.2

Where is the boss going to lunch?			
	Weight	Burger King	Subway
~~Boss always buys his lunch~~	~~L~~	~~+~~	~~+~~
Wife is monitoring his diet	H	-	+
Boss is thrifty	M	-	+
Dr. advises boss to eat right	H	-	+
~~Only two restaurants nearby~~	~~L~~	~~+~~	~~+~~

Step 5: Draw tentative conclusions about the relative likelihood of each hypothesis. Proceed by trying to disprove hypotheses rather than prove them.

Unlike step three which focused on evaluating the evidence, now review each hypothesis, moving *down* the columns of the matrix. In order to evaluate the likelihood of competing hypotheses, look for evidence or logical deductions that eliminate one or more hypothesis. Remember, information can be consistent with a number of hypotheses, so one should not necessarily choose the one with the most information *confirming* it. Rather, the analyst should concentrate on rejecting hypotheses when the collected information *disproves* it, and in the end, the matrix will only support the most likely hypothesis. Ignoring supporting evidence, Heuer claims that, "The hypothesis with the fewest minuses is probably the most likely one. The hypothesis with the most minuses is probably the least likely one."[59]

Where is the boss going to lunch? (Continued...) Step 5

Through the deductive process of the first four steps, the analyst is likely to begin to lean towards the hypothesis indicating that the boss is more likely to go to lunch at Subway. Looking at the matrix, Burger King received three minuses compared to zero assigned to Subway. Because the evidence serves to eliminate all but the most likely remaining hypothesis, Burger King appears to have been ruled out, leaving Subway as the most likely option.

However, this initial evaluation of the evidence and the accompanying notation is only a rough estimate. Some evidence is obviously more important than other evidence, which a single plus or minus cannot clearly represent. The purpose of the matrix is to guide the analyst to key elements and identify how these factors relate to the probability of each hypothesis, not to support the expected conclusion. In addition to serving as an analytic tool that objectively identifies all of the alternatives, Analysis of Competing Hypotheses serves as a record of the analytic process and an audit trail illustrating the steps by which the analyst arrived at the final estimate.

Step 6: Analyze how sensitive your conclusion is to a few critical items of evidence. Consider the consequences for your analysis if that evidence were wrong, misleading, or subject to a different interpretation.

In this step, re-examine the key assumptions and pieces of evidence that seem to drive the analysis in a particular direction. Single out the piece(s) of evidence that are most influential in causing rejection of one or more hypothesis. This is the stage at which challenging key assumptions may alter the entire process. It is also an appropriate time to consider the possibility of deception having been incorporated into the evidence.

Where is the boss going to lunch? (Continued...)
Step 6

Re-examine the key pieces of evidence driving rejection of the Burger King hypothesis.
   Despite the boss's love for French fries, high cholesterol and elevated blood pressure incline him toward Subway as the better choice to comply with doctor's orders to avoid fatty foods. In addition, the boss does not want to upset his domineering wife who monitors his daily dietary choices. Therefore, Subway remains the more competitive of the two hypotheses.

Step 7: Report conclusions. Discuss the relative likelihood of each hypothesis, not just the most likely one.

Decisionmakers should know the probability ranking of all of the hypotheses considered because analytic conclusions are never certain. Decisionmakers need to make decisions on the basis of all the alternative possibilities considered, and not just on a single hypothesis, in case they need a contingency or fallback plan.

Remember, when performing ACH, the analyst should proceed by *rejecting* hypotheses rather than *confirming* them. So it is important that the final product reflect that certain hypotheses were rejected and the reasons behind the selection of the most likely hypothesis so that decisionmakers can understand the logic behind the estimate.

Step 8: Identify milestones for future observations that may indicate events are taking a different course than expected.

Because events are dynamic and subject to a variety of influences, analytic conclusions are tentative. Therefore, it is useful to specify in advance that certain occurrences, if observed, could cause significant changes in the probability of the accepted or alternative hypotheses.

> **Where is the boss going to lunch? (Continued...)**
> **Step 8**
>
> Although the ACH process has led the weatherman to infer that the boss is most likely to go to Subway, it is *possible* that the overpowering aroma of French fries may change his mind, and he will go to Burger King, defying the estimate. Thus it is only "likely" that the boss will go to Subway.

Strengths

Heuer's Analysis of Competing Hypotheses helps analysts overcome cognitive biases, limitations, mindsets, and perceptions by testing multiple hypotheses at once. Typically, analysts identify what appears to be the most promising hypothesis before collecting and organizing information, and the analyst anticipates that the data will support the expected outcome. Heuer describes this as "satisficing" and claims that it is one of the major analytic stumbling blocks.[60] With ACH, an analyst can identify a number of credible hypotheses. By considering several hypotheses at once, the analyst will be unable to focus too much attention on a single outcome until all other possibilities are disproved. Moreover, when new information or evidence is collected, the analyst, using ACH, is able to change the estimate if the evidence is no longer supportive of the original conclusion.

Historically, analytic errors occur when something unexpected happens, and a decisionmaker wants an immediate estimate before sufficient information is available. Analysts often prepare estimates based on assumptions from historical examples and incomplete information, which, in time, may prove insufficient. However, the tendency to rely on mindsets and past assumptions is powerful and highly resistant to change;[61] the analyst will often reject information that does not fit the old model and will then generate inappropriate hypotheses leading to incorrect or incomplete estimative products. Again, using ACH forces the analyst to look at alternative hypotheses, thus ensuring the imaginative analyst is able to change his initial assessment. In addition, ACH prompts analysts to become aware of how dependent they may be on a single piece of evidence, which may have led them to the wrong conclusion.

Another strength of ACH is that it allows analysts to leave an audit trail unlike any other decisionmaking process. In the third step, analysts are required to construct a matrix listing hypotheses horizontally and evidence vertically. By listing the evidence, weighting its relevance and importance, and applying it to the hypotheses in the matrix, a record is created so that anyone can follow the evidence trail and thought processes that led to one conclusion or another. If there is a future question about the estimate, opposing parties can go back into the matrix and easily understand the process.

Weaknesses

Although Analysis of Competing Hypotheses is a valuable analytic tool, there are some intrinsic weaknesses in the methodology. Traditionally, when analysts perform ACH, they constructed a matrix using pen and paper. This process is long and arduous, especially when there are numerous hypotheses and a large body of evidence. Due to the amount of time that it takes to do this by hand and the time pressures that analysts usually encounter, the method is not applied as often as might be appropriate. For this reason, automation of ACH is critical and will be discussed in Chapter 5.

Another weakness of ACH is that it provides only a snapshot in time. The evidence used in the analysis is static, while events are dynamic. In order to provide a timely analytic product, analysts must determine a point at which to halt collection in order to prepare the estimate.

As is the case with any estimative product, analysis is only as good as the evidence that is included in the process. Unreliable evidence can undermine even the most thoughtful process execution. Also, because evidence can be ambiguous and prone to the pitfalls of deceptive tactics, it is difficult to determine the reliability and validity of the inputs.

Also, as Heuer admits, when used properly, ACH greatly reduces the effects of cognitive biases, mindsets, and perceptions, but can not completely eliminate them.

The degree to which ACH can reduce cognitive biases reflects the skill and imagination of the analyst using it. An analyst may value one piece of evidence over another and possibly weigh it more than a piece of evidence that is truly more valuable to an accurate estimate Also, an analyst may unconsciously gather more evidence in a particular category over another due to a particular field of expertise. For example, if one is preparing a report on the fate of Denmark's plastics industry, an economics expert might gather more specific detail on Denmark's economy rather than government regulations regarding the transportation of hazardous chemicals used in the production process. A reliance on one area of information may skew the estimate towards a particular hypothesis that would have not been chosen if all of the information were considered equally valuable.

In addition to preexisting mindsets, cultural biases may also hinder accurate estimate formation. Cultural biases must be considered when listing evidence and assumptions. An example of intelligence failure, due in part, to cultural bias, stems from American intelligence collection prior to the Japanese attack on Pearl Harbor. It is now believed that intelligence analysts grossly underestimated Japanese capabilities by viewing them from an American perspective.[62]

Although a fundamental purpose of ACH is to eliminate cognitive biases and mindsets, an analyst using this method might subconsciously still incorporate biases into the evaluation of the evidence.

Chapter 5: Structured Analysis of Competing Hypotheses

"A systematic process is the most effective way to facilitate good analysis. The non-structured approach has become the norm in the Intelligence Community. However, research shows that 'doing something systematic is better in almost all cases than seat-of-the-pants prediction'."
– Sundri Khalsa, The MITRE Corporation[63]

From the discussion of Analysis of Competing Hypotheses (ACH) weaknesses in Chapter 4, it is evident that the methodology lacks two key elements: structure and automation. Heuer's process has proven effective over the years, but it is tedious and time-consuming without automation and adding structure can enhance its effectiveness as an analytic tool.

Structure

Consider the phrase "DO GEESE SEE GOD." Whom might one ask for help in analyzing this phrase? A theologian? An ornithologist? Maybe a philosopher? How about a ninth grade English teacher – the person who first teaches us about palindromes. The Merriam-Webster dictionary defines palindromes as: "a word, verse, sentence, or a number that reads the same backward or forward."[64] Notice that this phrase reads the same forward and backward. However, if one does not immediately recognize this phrase as a palindrome, but assumes it is a question, the problem will be difficult to solve.

Conversely, if you imagine a Russian cryptologist unfamiliar with latinic script, you might also imagine someone who would seize upon the pattern first rather than focusing on the English language meaning of the phrase, thereby recognizing the palindrome much more rapidly. Taking a simpler, less sophisticated approach, in fact, yields a quicker, more conclusive answer.

To overcome this cognitive bias, Structured Analysis of Competing Hypotheses (SACH) helps the analyst to begin with the simplest hypotheses. SACH is an adaptation of the scientific method and follows from Heuer's Analysis of Competing Hypotheses (ACH) eight-step process. SACH begins with the simplest estimative hypothesis and drills downward, becoming increasingly specific, expanding and deepening the estimative conclusion.

The structure this method imposes upon ACH adds value by increasing the information provided in the final estimate. ACH may tell a decisionmaker that Usama bin Ladin intends to attack the US, but SACH is capable of telling him that he will do it in the next three months, using civilian aircraft, on the East Coast – as long as the evidence is robust and reliable enough to provide this level of estimation.

In this way, an analyst can split a single hypothesis into more complex hypotheses, which, once tested against the evidence, may be broken down even further[65]:

H 1:   Iraq has WMD
H 2:   Iraq does not have WMD

If the evidence indicated that there were WMD in Iraq, an analyst using SACH would then drill down further, forming these hypotheses:

H 1:   Iraq has WMD

H 1.1: WMD are in Baghdad
H 1.2: WMD are in Mosul

The analyst might also structure the initial ACH matrix by breaking down the original hypothesis that Iraq has WMD:

H 1:   Iraq has biological WMD

H 2:   Iraq has chemical WMD

H 3:   Iraq has nuclear WMD

Applying the analytic process numerous times to the same question affords the analyst the opportunity for greater nuance in their estimates while not having to increase the amount of evidence collected. In this way, the analyst gets the most robust estimate possible that is justified by the evidence available.

In addition, SACH is also an extremely valuable tool for providing

in defending estimates during evaluation. The methodology's structure enables an evaluator to view a clear audit trail from hypothesis generation, evidence collection, and application, throughout the analytic process. This clearly demonstrates that the estimate is the result of a thorough examination of all possible scenarios and a complete exploitation of available evidence.

Automation

One drawback of SACH is that the complexity of the methodology demands far more time than most analysts can afford. Thus, automation software greatly reduces the length of time it takes to complete the process. Numerous programs support the automation needed for structured analysis, including:

- DecisionBreakthrough
- Decide
  - o http://www.decide-tech.com
- Spotfire: DecisionSite
  - o http://www.spotfire.com

Using these tools to upload data into a matrix enables the analyst to organize his or her thoughts more easily. The software allows one to easily change how data is categorized: by hypotheses, relevance, or weight. In addition, the software strengthens the matrix by allowing the analyst to add, remove, or otherwise manipulate evidence and weights. Some products have a feature that calculates the degree of uncertainty in the evidence and highlights it for the analyst. The underlying algorithms in the program compute these bias alerts, assigning numeric values to the various coding mechanisms such as weights, and pluses and minuses. When the program detects an anomaly or high statistical variance, bias alerts draw attention to these outliers, or bias indicators, making the analyst aware of the areas that require further scrutiny or additional evidence. In other words, the outliers act as valuable pieces of evidence themselves.

Methodology

The structured part of SACH wraps around Heuer's eight-step process. The analyst starts with the simplest set of hypotheses possible. For example, imagine a country study. A good example of a simple hypothesis in this case might be "the country is stable" or, alternatively, "the country is unstable."

The next step is to see if ACH delivers a clear estimate. Imagine that all of the evidence clearly points to instability. With that clear estimate as background, the next step would be to broaden or deepen the tested hypotheses. In the case of the imaginary country study, the next step would be to form two or more new hypotheses about how the instability might manifest itself. So, for example, the instability might manifest itself in the form of a coup, or riots in the street, or just "muddling along." Again, the analyst tests the hypotheses against the *existing* evidence. Again, if there is a clear estimative answer, then the analyst forms a new set of hypotheses drilling down into the deepest estimative conclusion. Imagine the most recent test delivered a clear estimative judgment that there would be a coup. Then the analyst might dig even deeper into the available evidence to see if it said something about who might lead the coup.

Imagine, though, that at this level the evidence fails – an analysis of competing hypotheses of the three most likely leaders of the coup yields inconclusive estimates. This is a signal that the analyst has gone as deep as he or she can go with the evidence at hand. The next task is to target additional collection. The collection, of course, would be focused on either the hypotheses at hand (who might lead the coup) or it would be focused on resolving inconsistencies at this or other levels of the structure.

This structure works well with the Subway analysis discussed previously. Beginning with the final ACH hypothesis: the boss will have lunch at Subway, the analyst then asks himself if this is as far he can take the estimate, or can he provide something more specific? Specifically, at what time will the boss eat lunch at Subway? Once the analyst is able to determine the direction of the new hypothesis (i.e. the boss will eat at Subway at 1 p.m., not at noon), he or she will attempt to drill down into the estimate even further – as far as the availability of reliable evidence permits (see Figure 5.1).

Figure 5.1
Structured Analysis of Competing Hypotheses Flow Chart

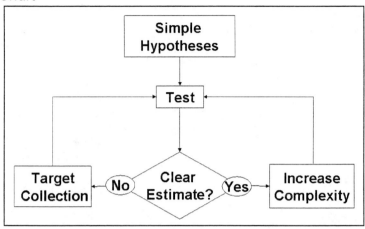

It is often also necessary to review the data and consider collecting additional evidence to provide a deeper level of analysis. Once the analyst has gathered additional data, the analyst repeats the process until the evidence is exhausted.

This process does not have a given end-point (see Figure 5.1). The analyst must determine the limits of his analytic ability to produce reliable estimates based on available evidence and halt the process in time to produce the final estimative product. Without this end-point, analysts might become merely reporters, providing information on events that have already taken place, rather than anticipating them with actionable information.

What time is the boss going to lunch?

In Chapter 4, the Analysis of Competing Hypotheses estimated that it was likely that the boss would go to Subway for lunch. However, new evidence might require a restructuring of the matrix. While getting coffee during the 10:00 break, the weatherman picked up the local newspaper and saw a front page article reporting a kitchen fire at Burger King late last night. As a result, Burger King is closed indefinitely for repairs. This means that the weatherman now has to go to Subway for lunch; even though his boss is likely to go there, too. However, the weatherman also has two additional pieces of information:

- The boss went to a meeting at 11:30, there is no telling how long he will be there, but lunch at 12:00 seems less certain now.
- The boss normally eats a late breakfast.

Now, using SACH, the weatherman must go further than his original ACH estimate and try to determine *what time* the boss is more likely to go to Subway for lunch. Based on previous experience, the weatherman can reliably conclude that the boss likes to go to lunch on the hour, usually at 12:00 or 1:00. Thus, he is able to create two new hypotheses:

- Boss will go to lunch at 12:00
- Boss will go to lunch at 1:00

Then, using DecisionBreakthrough software as an automation tool, he populates the matrix with the additional information, while changing the hypotheses along the top. Figure 5.2 illustrates the new matrix.

What time is the boss going to lunch? (Continued...)

Figure 5.2
SACH Matrix Using DecisionBreakthrough

Factors	Weight ⬇	The boss will go to Subway at 12:00	The boss will go to Subway at 1:00
Alternatives ➡			
The boss always buys lunch	L	+	+
Wife is monitoring diet	L	N	N
The boss is thrifty	L	N	N
The boss' Dr. says eat right	L	N	N
Only two restaurants nearby	L	N	N
The boss likes French fries	L	N	N
Fire at Burger King this morning	M	N	N
At 11:30 the boss is called upstairs to a meeting	M	–	+
Boss always eats a late breakfast	M	–	+

Following the addition of evidence into the new matrix, the weatherman must re-evaluate the evidence against the two new hypotheses. After this he determines that the evidence refutes the hypothesis "Boss will go to Subway at 12:00." As a result, the weatherman is able to estimate that it is highly likely that the boss will go to lunch at Subway at 1:00. The hungry weatherman will have to go to lunch at Subway before 1:00.

Note: DecisionBreakthrough is developed by Willard Zangwill, Professor, Graduate School of Business, University of Chicago, 2005.

Chapter 6: Presenting Analysis For A Decisionmaker

"If it is not intelligent and understandable, it is useless"
– Harry S. Truman, 34ᵗʰ President of the United States[66]

After the analyst has finalized an estimate, whether using Structured Analysis of Competing Hypotheses (or any other methodology), how does he or she transfer the information from the matrix, to a written report, and then to the decisionmaker? It is imperative that the analyst knows how to communicate the estimate most effectively to the decisionmaker for it to be of any value.

In their 2005 book, *Communicating With Decisionmakers,* Kristan Wheaton and Jennifer Wozny[67] have identified key elements decisionmakers prefer to see in reports prepared by intelligence analysts. These fourteen "maxims" are more than rules; they are cornerstones for effective communication between the analyst and the decisionmaker. Each maxim describes a different area of focus to improve communication but all of them are applicable to estimates reached through SACH.

Fourteen Maxims For Intelligence Analysis[68]

Maxim #1 BLUF – Bottom Line Up Front
Maxim #2 Consistency – Standardized terminology
Maxim #3 Novelty – New and insightful information
Maxim #4 Concision – Careful, efficient word choice
Maxim #5 Clarity – Clear and straightforward; no spelling or grammatical errors
Maxim #6 Accountability – Personal responsibility borne by analyst
Maxim #7 Accuracy – Accurate process and product; reliable sources
Maxim #8 Decisionmaker-focused – BLUF and document tailored to their needs
Maxim #9 Options – Alternatives and options clearly presented
Maxim #10 Unbiased – Honest and unbiased intelligence
Maxim #11 Packaging – Attractive, user-friendly packaging
Maxim #12 Timely – Timely intelligence
Maxim #13 Close Relationships – Close relationships between decisionmakers and analysts
Maxim #14 Informality – Shift toward informal, real-time analytic insights

Maxim #1 Bottom Line Up Front

According to the Sherman Kent School of Intelligence Analysis, "DI [Directorate of Intelligence] writing style emphasizes the bottom line up front, precise and concise language, and a clear articulation of our judgments and our confidence in them."[69]

The first thing a decisionmaker reads in an analytic report should be the bottom line right up front. This is best achieved with an executive summary – a short paragraph or three bullets pinpointing the estimate's key findings. This section should express the deepest level of estimation the analyst was able to achieve using the SACH tool.

Maxim #2 Consistency

As discussed in Chapter 2, standardized use of words of estimative probability (WEP) provides a clear assessment of the estimative outcome or options presented to the decisionmaker in terms he can clearly understand within a reasonable level of ambiguity. As the use of SACH increases analytic confidence, the analyst can easily apply WEP to his estimate to clarify the degree of certainty he has achieved performing this logical process.

Maxim #3 Novelty

"Several decisionmakers highlighted the fact that they are more knowledgeable on events and issues than analysts think."[70] For this reason, Wheaton and Wozny recommend that the analyst go beyond what the decisionmaker has requested and provide information that is useful but that the decisionmaker may not have thought to request.[71] This requires creativity, and the ability of analysts to think "outside the box," which are also necessary skills for imaginative hypothesis generation when using SACH. Endnotes also provide an excellent way to add information without overburdening the decisionmaker.

Maxim #4 Concision

Analysts should recognize that the purpose of creating an intelligence product is not to display their knowledge in a particular area. Rather, the purpose is to provide the necessary information for a decisionmaker to take a course of action or not. Decisionmakers are very busy and do not have time to read pages of data to get to the point; therefore, the product must be succinct for the decisionmaker to quickly and easily get the point of the estimate, such as providing only the final estimate derived from SACH with full information.

Maxim #5 Clarity

"The second most common issue decisionmakers discuss is their desire for a clear, straightforward, basic wording in intelligence documents."[72] Again, analysts have to make clear what they are trying to report and also illustrate what are facts, assumptions, and uncertainty in their estimate. Structured Analysis of Competing Hypotheses and the use of words of estimative probability prove their value by removing ambiguity and clearly identifying what is concrete evidence and what is an assumption. In addition, this process reduces uncertainty by organizing hypotheses and evidence in a logical manner, and drilling down to the most important element(s) of the estimate.

Maxim #6 Accountability

The Final Report of the Congressional Joint Inquiry into 9/11 strongly advised the Intelligence Community (IC) to implement measures guaranteeing accountability: "Assured standards of accountability are critical to developing the personal responsibility, urgency, and diligence which our counterterrorism responsibility requires."[73] This pressure for improved accountability affects both the analyst and the decisionmaker. Methodologies like SACH, when properly performed, can greatly increase the degree of accountability in the analytic process. Additionally, the decisionmaker can easily follow the series of matrices to ensure that the process is true, providing a reliable product.

Maxim #7 Accuracy

Two elements contribute to the accuracy of an intelligence estimate: process and product. An accurate process reflects the analyst's logical and relatively bias-free approach to the analysis, which combines with source reliability and effective presentation of the estimate to create an accurate product.[74] Lisa Krizan, in *Intelligence Essentials For Everyone,* presented in 1999 at the Joint Military Intelligence College in Washington DC claims, "Three aspects to consider in evaluating the relevance of information sources are reliability, proximity, and appropriateness. Reliability of a source is determined through an evaluation of its past performance. Proximity refs to the source's closeness to the information. Appropriateness of the source rests upon whether the source speaks from a position of authority on the specific issue in question."[75]

Maxim #8 Decisionmaker-focused

Analysts should always tailor their analysis to the decisionmaker or audience that has requested the product. Decisionmakers may view non-customized products as irrelevant, creating a communications failure, according to Walter Laquer, Chairman of Georgetown University's International Research Council of the Center for Strategic and International Studies. Analysts should modify intelligence products as prompted by previous decisionmaker's feedback for both form and content.

Maxim #9 Options

It is important to provide a decisionmaker with a full set of alternatives for them to take appropriate actions. However, an analyst must never provide "policy recommendations." Paul Wolfowitz, former Deputy Secretary of Defense, suggests that analysts should clearly articulate estimates but not "usurp the decision role of policymakers by prematurely limiting the options on the table."[76] Analysis of Competing Hypotheses (ACH) and SACH allows the analyst to formulate a full set of alternative hypotheses by considering as many outcomes as cannot be disproved and comparing them further with evidence collected. The audit trail that accompanies this methodology allows the decisionmaker to review all of the hypotheses and feel more confident that the analyst has done a thorough job of weighing all options.

Maxim #10 Unbiased

Finally, analysts should provide decisionmakers with objective and unbiased intelligence, free from personal opinions and debilitating mindsets. Similar to Maxim #5, analysts should clearly identify any assumptions or preconceptions that they have permitted to affect the analysis. ACH and SACH methodology are designed specifically to combat the detrimental effects of cognitive biases.

Preparing intelligence for decisionmakers is more than just knowing or even understanding the above maxims. There is no substitute for actually putting the results of considered intelligence analysis out for decisionmakers to use and evaluate. Utilizing these guidelines, in short, does not guarantee successful communication with decisionmakers; it only increases the chances of such communication.

Maxim #11 Tailor-Made Packaging

Analysts should use decisionmaker feedback as a method to tailor future products, as well as incorporate feedback into product planning. As analysts need to understand what their decisionmakers want in order to produce good intelligence, close involvement between the decisionmaker and analyst when making the requirement produces one that is sufficiently detailed. Further, analysts with good cognitive abilities can better comprehend and discern what decisionmakers want and guide them to producing sufficiently specific and detailed requirements.

Maxim #12 Timely

Intelligence is only useful if it is timely. We can define "timely" in two ways, the first meaning simply "on time". For a decisionmaker with a 0900 meeting, receiving key information by 0859 is essential; after 0900, the data is too late. On another level, timeliness means simply "in advance," and is a key facet of good intelligence.

Maxim #13 Close Personal Relationships

It may seem surprising to note how many decisionmakers wanted close relationships with their analysts. To explain, if a report comes across your desk from someone of whom you have never heard, you may read it and consider its conclusions, but you are less likely to give weight to them. Conversely, you are more likely to put stock in a report from your good friend Joe Analyst, whose credibility level you have determined. In the latter case, you will be comfortable that if Joe says "highly likely," then it is "highly likely," because you know that Joe chooses his words very carefully.

Close relationships also benefit the requirements phase, allowing analysts to ensure their tasks are detailed and specific to the customer's needs. The contact also allows both parties to ask follow-up questions or give or request feedback.

Maxim #14 Informal Intelligence

Perhaps a newly emerging theme among decisionmakers is their preference for and reliance on less-formalized intelligence forms. Lisa Krizan attributes this shift in delivery methods to technological evolution, and feels such methods will likely continue to change as time goes on.

A handful of decisionmakers cited above explicitly recognize the value in real-time, as-needed, "raw" intelligence reports. That is, they like the idea of calling or emailing their analyst to pose a quick question, or meeting the analyst in the hallway to spend a few minutes discussing an issue of concern to the decisionmaker.

Annex 1: Presidential Daily Brief, 06 August 2001

Bin Ladin Determined To Strike in US

Clandestine, foreign government, and media reports indicate Bin Ladin since 1997 has wanted to conduct terrorist attacks in the US. Bin Ladin implied in US television interviews in 1997 and 1998 that his followers would follow the example of World Trade Center bomber Ramzi Yousel and "bring the fighting to America."

After US missile strikes on his base in Afghanistan in 1998, Bin Ladin told followers he wanted to retaliate in Washington, according to a ███████████████ service.

An Egyptian Islamic Jihad (EIJ) operative told an███████ service at the same time that Bin Ladin was planning to exploit the operative's access to the US to mount a terrorist strike.

The millennium plotting in Canada in 1999 may have been part of Bin Ladin's first serious attempt to implement a terrorist strike in the US. Convicted plotter Ahmed Ressam has told the FBI that he conceived the idea to attack Los Angeles International Airport himself, but that Bin Ladin lieutenant Abu Zubaydah encouraged him and helped facilitate the operation. Ressam also said that in 1998 Abu Zubaydah was planning his own US attack.

Ressam says Bin Ladin was aware of the Los Angeles operation.

Although Bin Ladin has not succeeded, his attacks against the US Embassies in Kenya and Tanzania in 1998 demonstrate that he prepares operations years in advance and is not deterred by setbacks. Bin Ladin associates surveilled our Embassies in Nairobi and Dar es Salaam as early as 1993, and some members of the Nairobi cell planning the bombings were arrested and deported in 1997.

Al-Qa'ida members—including some who are US citizens—have resided in or traveled to the US for years, and the group apparently maintains a support structure that could aid attacks. Two al-Qa'ida members found guilty in the conspiracy to bomb our Embassies in East Africa were US citizens, and a senior EIJ member lived in California in the mid-1990s.

A clandestine source said in 1998 that a Bin Ladin cell in New York was recruiting Muslim-American youth for attacks.

We have not been able to corroborate some of the more sensational threat reporting, such as that from a ███████████████ *service in 1998 saying that Bin Ladin wanted to hijack a US aircraft to gain the release of "Blind Shaykh" 'Umar 'Abd al-Rahman and other US-held extremists.*

continued

- 70 -

— Nevertheless, FBI information since that time indicates patterns of suspicious activity in this country consistent with preparations for hijackings or other types of attacks, including recent surveillance of federal buildings in New York.

The FBI is conducting approximately 70 full field investigations throughout the US that it considers Bin Ladin-related. CIA and the FBI are investigating a call to our Embassy in the UAE in May saying that a group of Bin Ladin supporters was in the US planning attacks with explosives.

- 71 -

Annex 2: Oral Presentation Recommendations

Aside from producing written analytic reports in which analysts focus largely on content, effective communication requires analysts to be able to brief their decisionmakers as well. The following guidelines are recommended by Wheaton and Wozny[77] as those most important to the decisionmakers they have surveyed:

Preparation:
The analyst must be well prepared and have a firm grasp of all relevant facts.

Electronic Media:
The technology must be appropriate and the briefer must be skilled in its use.

Spelling And Grammar:
The presentation should be error free and the presenter should use correct and consistent pronunciation (i.e. foreign names and locations).

Time:
The presentation should go no more or less than the allotted time.

Identify Self:
The presenter should clearly state their name, title, and the purpose of the briefing.

Engage Audience:
The briefer must capture the attention of the audience from the start and hold it throughout the presentation.

Organized Content:
The content must be clear, logical, and organized

Transitions:
The presenter must have smooth transitions between topics and slides.

Visual Aids And Examples:
The presentation should contain helpful and well-designed graphics that aid the presentation and not distract the audience.

Closing Comments:
Closing comments should be concise, well thought-out, and add value to the presentation.

Thank You:
The presenter should take the time to briefly, but genuinely, thank the audience.

Questions:
The presenter should always ask for questions, even if no one immediately asks a question. The briefer should not leave, but give them a little time so as not to appear to be avoiding questions.

Eye Contact:

Provide consistent, engaging, and evenly-distributed eye contact.

Gestures:

Subtle hand gestures should be used to add to and not detract from the presentation, almost blending into the background.

Vocal Quality And Pace:

Vocal quality should be clear and audible. The pace should engage the audience to keep them interested.

Energy And Enthusiasm:

The presenter should emit a contagious enthusiasm, showing that one has a clear interest in the topic and in the presentation.

Poise And Confidence:

The presenter should display a balanced and professional confidence in the subject.

Personal Appearance:

The presenter should be well groomed and dressed appropriately for the occasion, depending on the subject and the audience.

Annex 3: SACH Addresses Recommendations Of Recent Intelligence Reviews

Below are recommendations from both of the recent reports addressing current shortcomings in the US Intelligence Community (IC) in assessing and communicating threats to US national security. Structured Analysis of Competing Hypotheses (SACH) can provide solutions to the problems prompting these recommendations.

WMD Report Recommendations:[78]

1. The Community must develop and integrate into regular use new tools to assist analysts in filtering and correlating the vast quantities of information that threaten to overwhelm the analytic process. Moreover, data from all sources of information should be processed and correlated Community-wide before being conveyed to analysts. (402)

2. A new long-term research analysis unit, under the mantle of the National Intelligence Council, should wall off all-source analysts from daily demands and serve as the lead organization for interagency projects involving in-depth analysis. (403)

3. The [Directorate of National Intelligence] DNI should encourage diverse and independent analysis throughout the Intelligence Community by encouraging alternative hypothesis generation as part of the analytic process and by forming offices dedicated to independent analysis. (405)

4. The Intelligence Community must develop a Community program for training analysts, and both analysts and managers must prioritize this career-long training. (409)

5. The Intelligence Community must develop a Community program for training managers, both when they first assume managerial positions and throughout their careers. (410)

6. Finished intelligence should include careful sourcing for all analytic assessments, and such materials should – whenever possible in light of legitimate security concerns – be made easily available to intelligence customers. (412)

7. The analytic community should create and store sourced copies of all analytic pieces to allow readers to locate and review the intelligence upon which analysis is based, and to allow for easy identification of analysis that is based on intelligence reports that are later modified. (413)

8. The DNI should explore ways to make finished intelligence available to customers in a way that enables them – to the extent they desire – to more easily find pieces of interest, link to related materials, and communicate with analysts. (417)

9. Examinations of finished intelligence should be routine and ongoing, and the lessons learned from the "post mortems" should be incorporated into the intelligence education and training program. (425)

9/11 Commission Report Recommendations:[79]

1. Information procedures should provide incentives for sharing, to restore a better balance between security and shared knowledge. (417)

2. The president should lead the government-wide effort to bring the major national security institutions into the information revolution. He should coordinate the resolution of the legal, policy, and technical issues across agencies to create a "trusted information network." (418)

3. Congressional oversight for intelligence – and counterterrorism – is now dysfunctional. Congress should address this problem. We have considered various alternatives: A joint committee on the old model of the Joint Committee on Atomic Energy is one. A single committee in each house of Congress, combining authorizing and appropriating authorities, is another. (420)

4. Congress should create a single, principal point of oversight and review for homeland security. Congressional leaders are best able to judge what committee should have jurisdiction over this department and its duties. But we believe that Congress does have the obligation to choose one in the House and one in the Senate, and that this committee should be a permanent standing committee with a nonpartisan staff. (421)

Acknowledgements

Jim Breckenridge inspired the concept of adding structure to Richards Heuer's brilliant original methodology of Analysis of Competing Hypotheses, making Heuer's important contribution even more valuable to the analytic field. Special thanks go to William Welch for his assistance in editing and his firm stand on issues of punctuation which enhanced the presentation of source material. In addition to her invaluable contribution to the original writing of the text, Katrina Altman provided excellent assistance in fact verification, in compiling the index, as well as in improving the overall format of the final volume.

Kris Wheaton thanks the wonderful students of Mercyhurst College who have contributed to the increased understanding of intelligence theory and the processes that surround it. He would also like to thank his wife, Judy and his children, Charlie and Joe, for their patience and support.

Diane Chido expresses her thanks to her family who supported her throughout her work at Mercyhurst, and especially her son, Zachary, for his patience while mom was working.

Index

Endnotes

[1] Richards J. Heuer, Jr., *Psychology of Intelligence Analysis*. (Washington D.C.: CIA Center for the Study of Intelligence, 1999), 4.

[2] Malcolm Gladwell, Blink: *The Power of Thinking Without Thinking*. (New York: Little, Brown, and Company, 2005)

[3] Heuer, 111.

[4] A good example of such a bias is attentional blindness. This occurs when an analyst is hyper-focused on one aspect of the analysis and entirely misses a more important facet. For example, an analyst attending the May Day celebration in Red Square may be so busy counting the number of tanks, he or she may entirely miss that a key member of the government is missing from the review stand.

[5] Walter Laquer, *A World of Secrets: The Uses and Limits of Intelligence* (New York, NY: Basic Books, 1985), p 8.

[6] US House of Representatives, *Intelligence Reform and Terrorism Prevention Act of 2004*, 2004 <http://a255.g.akamaitech.net/7/255/2422/13dec20041150/www.gpoac cess.gov/serialset/creports/pdf/108-796/108-796_intel_reform.pdf> Accessed 20 June 2005.

[7] US Congress, *National Security Act Of 1947*, 1947 <http://www.iwar.org.uk/sigint/resources/national-security-act/1947-act.htm> Accessed 20 June 2005.

[8] Sherman Kent, *Strategic Intelligence For American World Policy* (Princeton: Princeton University Press, Princeton, 1949), 3.

[9] Kent, 69.

[10] Kent, 151.

[11] Mark M. Lowenthal, *Intelligence: From Secrets To Policy* (Washington D.C.: CQ Press, 2002), Back Cover.

[12] Lowenthal, 8.

[13] Lowenthal, 2.

[14] Robert M. Clark, *Intelligence Analysis: A Target-Centric Approach* (Washington D.C.: CQ Press, 2004), 13-14.

[15] Clark, 13

[16] Larry Kahaner, *Competitive Intelligence* (New York: Simon & Schuster, 1996), 16.

[17] Kahaner, 23-25.

[18] White House Transcript, President Bush's Address to the American People on 17 December 2004. President Bush signed the Intelligence Reform and Terrorism Prevention Act of 2004.

<http://www.whitehouse.gov/news/releases/2004/12/20041217-1.html>
Accessed 13 June 2005.
[19] Clark, 15.
[20] Clark, 16.
[21] Clark, 15-16.
[22] Clark, 14.
[23] Clark, 18.
[24] "Book: Bush Had Secret War Plan," *CBS News*, 16 April 2004,
<http://www.cbsnews.com/stories/2004/04/17/iraq/main612400.shtml>
Accessed 21 June 2005.
[25] Commission On The Intelligence Capabilities Of The United States
Regarding Weapons Of Mass Destruction, Report To The President Of
The United States, 31 March 2005 (Washington D.C, Introduction),
<http://www.wmd.gov/report/> Accessed 21 June 2005.
[26] Michael Warner, "Wanted: A Definition of 'Intelligence'," Studies
in Intelligence. 2002,
<http://www.cia.gov/csi/studies/vol46no3/article02.html> Accessed 20
June 2005.
[27] Commission On The Intelligence Capabilities Of The United States
Regarding Weapons Of Mass Destruction, Report To The President Of
The United States, 31 March 2005 (Washington D.C, 419),
<http://www.wmd.gov/report/> Accessed 21 June 2005.
[28] White House Press Fact Sheet accompanying release of declassified
6 August 2001 Presidential Daily Briefing Memo,
< http://www.fas.org/irp/news/2004/04/wh041004.html> Accessed 15
November 2005.
[29] Joseph Curl, "Bush Tells Panel Memo Lacked Menu," The
Washington Times, 30 April 2004,
< http://www.washtimes.com/national/20040429-113358-9307r.htm>
Accessed 20 June 2005.
[30] Presidential Daily Brief, bin *Ladin Determined To Strike In US*, 06
August 2001, Declassified and Approved 10 April 2004,
<http://www.gwu.edu/~nsarchiv/NSAEBB/NSAEBB116/pdb8-6-
2001.pdf>
Accessed 20 June 2005.
[31] Sherman, Kent, "Words of Estimative Probability," *Center For The
Study Of Intelligence*, 1964,
<http://www.cia.gov/csi/books/shermankent/6words.html> Accessed
20 June 2005.
[32] Sherman, Kent, "Words of Estimative Probability," *Center For The
Study Of Intelligence*, 1964,

<http://www.cia.gov/csi/books/shermankent/6words.html> Accessed 20 June 2005.

[33] Sherman, Kent, "Words of Estimative Probability," *Center For The Study Of Intelligence*, 1964, <http://www.cia.gov/csi/books/shermankent/6words.html> Accessed 20 June 2005.

[34] Sherman, Kent, "Words of Estimative Probability," *Center For The Study Of Intelligence*, 1964, <http://www.cia.gov/csi/books/shermankent/6words.html> Accessed 20 June 2005.

[35] Sherman, Kent, "Words of Estimative Probability," *Center For The Study Of Intelligence*, 1964, <http://www.cia.gov/csi/books/shermankent/6words.html> Accessed 20 June 2005.

[36] Sherman, Kent, "Words of Estimative Probability," *Center For The Study Of Intelligence*, 1964, <http://www.cia.gov/csi/books/shermankent/6words.html> Accessed 20 June 2005.

[37] [37] Sherman, Kent, "Words of Estimative Probability," *Center For The Study Of Intelligence*, 1964, <http://www.cia.gov/csi/books/shermankent/6words.html> Accessed 20 June 2005.

[38] Schrage.

[39] Michael Schrage, "What Percent Is Slam Dunk?; Give Us Odds on Those Estimates." *The Washington Post*, 20 February 2005, sec. B.

[40] Schrage.

[41] Inderjeet Mani and Gary L. Klein, "Evaluating Intelligence Analysis In Open-Ended Situations," The MITRE Corporation, 2-6 May 2005, <https://analysis.mitre.org/proceedings/Final_Papers_Files/189_Camer a_Ready_Paper.pdf> Accessed 20 June 2005.

[42] Radford M. Neal, "Philosophy Of Bayesian Inference," University of Toronto, January 1998, < http://www.cs.toronto.edu/~radford/res-bayes-ex.html> Accessed 20 June 2005.

[43] Lowenthal, 20.

[44] Richards J. Heuer, Jr., "Limits Of Intelligence Analysis," *Orbis,* Winter 2005, 75-94.

[45] Commission On The Intelligence Capabilities Of The United States Regarding Weapons Of Mass Destruction, Report To The President Of The United States, 31 March 2005 (Washington D.C, 405), <http://www.wmd.gov/report/> Accessed 21 June 2005.